EARLY AMERICAN INDIAN TRIBES

2nd Grade U.S. History Vol 4

Speedy Publishing LLC
40 E. Main St. #1156
Newark, DE 19711
www.speedypublishing.com

People lived in the United States long before the arrival of Christopher Columbus and the Europeans.

The first people to live in a land are called indigenous peoples.

The Native
Americans are
the indigenous
peoples of the
United States when
Europeans arrived.

Native Americans lived throughout North and South America. Different tribes and cultures lived in different areas.

These peoples are also referred to as Indians or American Indians.

Christopher Columbus was travelling west, so he thought he was going to India.

This is why he called the people "Indians".

The Native Americans were grouped into tribes based on the area they lived in and their culture.

All of the Native American tribes had some things in common. They lived by gathering food in the earliest times and then planting crops later in history.

The most important Native American food crop was corn, or what they called maize.

Maize was eaten by many of the American Indian tribes because it could be stored for the winter and ground into flour.

Native Americans lived in a wide variety of homes. Different tribes built different types of homes.

Some used portable structures that could be moved to follow the bison herds. They were called Teepees.

Prior to Europeans arriving and bringing horses with them, there weren't any horses in America.

When horses arrived, everything changed. Horses made it much easier to travel and hunt.

Music and dance were important parts of the Native American culture.There were hundreds of Dances that were performed by all the different tribes.

Dances were performed for a variety of reasons. It includes war dances, victory dances, fertility dances, homecoming dances and rain dances.

All Native American people were very spiritual and they had many religious rituals.

They believed in a special relationship with nature. They worshiped the sun because they needed it to grow their crops.

www.ingramcontent.com/pod-product-compliance
Lightning Source LLC
LaVergne TN
LVHW060510170826
845677LV00026B/1710
9798869449351